A Birder's Devotional
Backyard Edition

By Matthew D. Bennett

A Birder's Devotional: Backyard Edition
Published by Bird and the Word Press

All rights reserved

ISBN: 979-8-9989978-0-8

For Abi, Roeh, TD, and Josi.

Go find a bird.
- Daddy

Introduction

All through my life and Christian journey, I've always been fascinated by the beauty of all that God has created and His word. Birds, one of God's beautiful creations, are special to me. From their rhythmic sounds, appearance, colors and unique characteristics, they serve as a daily reminder to me of God's love, care, creativity and provision.

This daily devotional is a combination of two things that have become a great passion for me over the years-Scripture and birds. The Bible highlights Jesus' references to birds in His teachings about love, faith, trust and provision. I strongly believe that we can draw closer and have a deeper understanding of Him when we carefully look at these amazing creatures God has blessed us with.

Each day in this devotional will focus on different components of the bird, attributing its characteristics to messages in the Bible. My desire for you, the reader, is that you get a deeper knowledge of birds and will be inspired to appreciate the good works of God in our daily lives. Be encouraged to look deeper, observe and focus on the only One who knew you even before you were born.

So, whatever your daily routine is, make every effort to take the time to pay close attention to your environment, especially the birds, and to read the scripture and appreciate God for all He has done.

As we delve deeper, we'll begin to understand the lessons God has in store for us in the feathers and flight of our backyard neighbors.

Day 1
Northern Cardinal

"Look at the birds of the air; they do not sow or reap or store away in barns, and yet your heavenly Father feeds them. Are you not much more valuable than they?" – Matthew 6:26

Northern Cardinals are beautiful birds with red plumage often found in the neck of the woods all through North America. Cardinals are special birds with bright colors that set them apart from the environment, especially when they perch on green trees. Their beautiful colors are a reflection of the beauty of nature and its creativity, especially to the gardens they often dwell in.

Found in large numbers during spring, for many people cardinals embody a new beginning and renewed hope. The cardinal represents exactly what Jesus spoke of in Matthew 6:26, which says that if God can provide for the birds of the sky, how much more will He provide for us, whom He created in His image? The presence of cardinals in our backyards heightens our trust in God's provision, with the hope that all that we seek will be made available to us; to believe that our needs will be met; and to be aware of the blessings all around us.

Lord, we adore you for all the beautiful things you've blessed us with. The cardinal's song and color symbolize that beauty. Lord, strengthen our faith in Your provision so that we might rejoice in Your daily care for us. Amen.

Day 2
Ruby-crowned Kinglet

"But he said to me, 'My grace is sufficient for you, for my power is made perfect in weakness."
– 2 Corinthians 9:12

The Ruby-Crowned Kinglet, one of the smallest songbirds you can find in North America, is a small bird that poses a challenge to study due to its muted olive-green feathers. The male species of the bird displays a red crown that is only seen when excited. Despite its size, the little kinglet is an adaptive and strong bird. Their ability to thrive in such a variety of environments - from dense forests, to open woodlands, deserts, and suburban backyards - demonstrates how adaptable and tough they are.

Just like the kinglet, we have the strength to make decisions when it comes to our weaknesses. We either let them mar us or make us. In 2 Corinthians, the Apostle Paul mentioned that the things that hinder us can become an opportunity for God to manifest His glory in our lives. When God made man, He gave him the power to overcome challenges, which is proof that His love and strength are sufficient and are made perfect in our weakness. Hence, the secret to unlocking these potentials is by surrendering to Jesus, who leads us into all truth.

Lord, I bring forth my weaknesses unto thee in light of your glory. I cannot do it all on my own, but I know you are all-powerful and your grace is sufficient for me. Help me to always keep in mind that this glorious truth and may it motivate me to glorify You in my life today. Amen.

Day 3
American Robin

"Thus, by their fruit you will recognize them."
– Matthew 7:20

Known for its orange-colored belly and musical prowess, the American Robin is a bird popularly seen in backyards. Historically, it is believed that their appearance signifies the beginning of spring, even though they can be seen all through the different seasons of the year. Its unique characteristic is that it can survive even the toughest season. No matter the season, you can see the Robin showcasing its beauty. This is a wonderful reminder that God is present with us in every season of our lives.

The Bible teaches us that a disciple is recognizable by how they bear fruit. In the same way, a Robin can be easily recognized by its color and melodious song. We also are to be recognized by the fruits of our actions and attitudes. In His preaching, Jesus emphasized our love for one another as a sign that we are His disciples. In order to be fruitful, just as Christ had mentioned, we must learn to love.

Lord, let your grace be upon me today to help me bear good fruit. May your Spirit continue to lead me so that my words and actions reflect your love, and lead others to You. Amen.

Day 4

White-breasted Nuthatch

"I lift up my eyes to the hills. From where does my help come? My help comes from the Lord, who made heaven and earth." – Psalm 121:1-2

A unique feature that distinguishes the White-Breasted Nuthatch from other birds is its agility, which comes from the bird's ability to crack hard and large nuts to feast on the internal content. They also possess the ability to walk headfirst while descending tree trunks. They are tough birds that are unfazed by difficult challenges or uncharted territories as they trust in their instincts and move with energy and joy.

When we seek God's face in the midst of our troubles, He gives us the strength to face life's obstacles, just like the challenges that the White-Breasted Nuthatch face. When we are faced with life's uncertainties or even persecution, we must always remember where the source of our strength comes from. Solely depending on the Spirit's guidance to navigate these tough waters is the only way we can avoid being overwhelmed by these challenges. So, when you find yourself in the midst of challenges today, remember that your help comes from the Lord.

Thank you, God, for being my refuge and fortress. Help me to remember to always run to you when I am in need and faced with life's troubles. Thank you for giving me the strength to ascend and discover uncharted territories. Amen.

Day 5

House Finch

"Rejoice always, pray continually, give thanks in all circumstances; for this is God's will for you in Christ Jesus." – 1 Thessalonians 5:16-18

Another bird that can frequently be seen in backyards is the House Finch, which often visits feeders in large flocks. It is always a joy to see this bird, especially the male with its bright red plumage along its back. Their color and gregarious nature seem to liven up any environment. When it comes to choosing a home, the House Finch is not particularly picky. You can find them in rural and urban habitats alike.

Regardless of where they can be found, their demeanor seems to stay the same: bright and energetic. The House Finch can serve as a great reminder of the truths found in 1 Thessalonians 5:16-18: to be able to adapt and find joy in any number of circumstances; to be grateful and content in any and all circumstances. Seeing the world through this lens - of gratitude and contentment - will help our souls find rest. With an attitude of gratitude, we can find ways to glorify God as we walk through every season of life. As you face challenges today, strive to find contentment and look for a reason to give thanks to God.

Father, I just want to say thank you. You are the giver of all good things, and You are with me in every season. I recognize that I have a tendency to take my eyes off of You and get too fixated on my circumstances. Help me to remember You and what you have done in every moment. Amen

Day 6

Blue Jay

"Let your conversation be always full of grace, seasoned with salt, so that you may know how to answer everyone." – Colossians 4:6

The Blue Jay is a bold bird known for its dominating presence and loud, distinctive call. This bird is a backyard staple in much of North America. While its color and markings make it easily distinguishable, it is his voice that sets it apart. The Blue Jay's powerful call reminds us of the impact of our words. The Bible encourages us to carefully consider the use of our words. We have an opportunity every day to speak life to those we interact with. Just as salt is used to season and preserve, our words have the same ability.

Whether used positively or negatively, our words have the power to resonate with the world around us. It is often easy to speak in a reactionary manner without thinking or considering the effect of our words. It is also easy to put more emphasis on the volume of our words than the content. As followers of Christ, we are called to let our conversation be full of grace, choosing to edify and encourage. Be intentional with how you use your words today, and may they reflect the love and grace of God.

Lord, may you guide my words and interactions today. Help me to speak with grace and wisdom, using my voice in a positive way. Help me to use my voice to speak life into the world around me, pointing people to You. Amen.

Day 7

Pine Siskin

"Fear not, for I am with you; be not dismayed, for I am your God; I will strengthen you, I will help you, I will uphold you with my righteous right hand."
– Isaiah 41:10

The Pine Siskin is a small bird in the finch family. Look for its yellow and brown streaks as well as its forked tail in flight. Often seen in flocks, these tiny birds are a mainstay in backyards and coniferous forests alike, especially in the winter months. Their vivacious personality, typical of finches, infuses life into everything it touches.

The Pine Siskin teaches us a valuable lesson regarding community, emphasizing leaning on one another for support in times of trouble. A Pine Siskin on its own would be in trouble, and it's no different for us. We should lean on one another and bear with one another, always pointing each other to the Lord. He promises to strengthen and sustain us in every season if we seek Him. Let us strive to always be ready to encourage someone by reminding them of this truth.

Heavenly Father, thank you for being ever-present in my life. You are never far away. Help me to surround myself with a community that loves You and helps me to trust you more. Amen.

Day 8
Cedar Waxwing

"But the fruit of the Spirit is love, joy, peace, forbearance, kindness, goodness, faithfulness, gentleness, and self-control. Against such things there is no law." – Galatians 5:22-23

The Cedar Waxwing is a visually gorgeous bird that can match the color and elegance of exotic birds. Their silky, smooth complexion paired with their distinctive black mask makes them an amazing sight to behold. The Cedar Waxwing often forms large, unruly flocks and can be found year-round. This bird is also a fruit expert, often found perched atop various fruit trees, devouring berries whole. There is a great connection between the Cedar Waxwing and Paul's words in Galatians.

As followers of Jesus, we are reminded that we are have the fruit of the Spirit. This distinguishes us from the world around us. Where others may be controlled by their emotions or surroundings, we are prompted by the Spirit. The Holy Spirit helps the believer to respond with love, joy, peace, and beyond. Truth is, we don't have to walk and talk like the world around us. By His Spirit, we are able to bear fruit in every season.

Thank You, God, for your Spirit. I know that I am not able to bear good fruit on my own. Praise You for enabling me to live differently. Help me today to live according to Your will and point people to You by the way I live. May my life be an example of Your love. Amen.

Day 9

Scissor-tailed Flycatcher

"I will instruct you and teach you in the way you should go; I will counsel you with my loving eye on you." – Psalm 32:8

The Scissor-tailed Flycatcher is a breathtaking bird that is known by its absurdly long tail. With its elegant color pattern and graceful flight, this bird is easily recognizable. Often seen gliding and swooping through the air, the Flycatcher is the embodiment of freedom and grace. This bird thrives in open spaces, where it hunts insects and enjoys the warm sun, reminding us of the beauty of embracing the paths on which God has placed us.

Just as the flycatcher depends on its instinct while navigating the skies, we are called to rely on God's guidance instead of our own "knowledge." Psalm 32:8 reassures us that God is active in His creation. He is diligently instructing and counseling us, watching over us with love and protection. The Scissor-tailed Flycatcher motivates us to spread our wings, step out in faith, and embrace God's calling for our life. His loving eye is always on His children.

Lord, help me to trust in Your voice today. Open my heart and ears to hear your call clearly and grant me the confidence to follow where you lead. Amen.

Day 10
Red-winged Blackbird

"The Lord watches over you-the Lord is your shade at your right hand." – Psalm 121:5

One of the many birds that can be seen in almost every state is the Red-Winged Blackbird. This brightly colored bird is frequently seen atop cattails, along damp roadsides, and on telephone lines. They can also be found in large flocks, often mixed in with other birds like grackles and starlings. The red-winged blackbird is also a ferocious protector who frequently chases away other birds, larger animals, and even humans from its territory to showcase its dominance. This unique characteristic of theirs reminds us of how the Lord watches over and protects His children.

God's presence in our lives goes a step further. He doesn't simply watch from afar. He is active in His protection, always close enough to cover us in any trial. Just as the Red-winged Blackbird has a natural instinct to defend, God's character has the same track record. He is our refuge in every season, and we should depend solely on Him by trusting in His word. Scripture also points out that He gives us a peace that surpasses all understanding. So, when our flesh says to worry, we can remember that God is faithful to watch over and protect us, allowing us to have peace.

Heavenly Father, thank You for watching over me and being my fierce protector. Help me to remember to run to You first. I trust that you are always near and that I can find comfort in you. Guard me today. Amen.

Day 11
American Goldfinch

"The joy of the Lord is your strength."
– Nehemiah 8:10

The American Goldfinch is a beautiful bird that exudes joy and energy. This bird is a common sight in backyards, often seen feeding on the ground beneath bird feeders during the winter time. Their unique bouncing pattern in flight mimics that of a choreographed routine. Their unique flight pattern, when paired with their bright yellow feathers, makes them easily identifiable. Their lively presence brings joy to our lives and lawns alike.

It is inevitable that we all go through tough seasons and even dire circumstances, in our life's journey. If we try to find joy in our circumstances or other things that our world deems important, we are destined for a let-down. The demeanor of the American Goldfinch reminds us that we can find joy in the seemingly mundane. When we view God as our ultimate source of joy, this becomes much more attainable for us too. When we realize that the joy of the Lord is our strength, we can live joyfully beyond our circumstances. We should embrace each day with joy, much like the goldfinch. God's presence and promise allow us to face each day with a joyful and worshipful heart.

Lord, fill me with Your joy today. Make it my strength in all situations and may I show others Your light and love. Help my joy to be untethered to my circumstances today. Amen.

Day 12

Downy Woodpecker

"Let the favor of the Lord our God be upon us, and establish the work of our hands upon us; yes, establish the work of our hands." – Psalm 90:17

The Downy Woodpecker is a small member of the woodpecker family. What this bird lacks in size, it makes up for in energy and volume. Whether by their shrill call or the drumming of their beak, they ensure to make their presence known. Often seen scurrying around tree trunks, their persistent and diligent work portrays their commitment to the task at hand.

We, too, are called to approach our duties with determination and care. Doing this is easier said than done. However, when we seek the Lord, He promises to establish the work of our hands. This, in turn, positively affects the way in which we view even the most simple routines. By trusting in His provision and care, we can find fulfillment in our labor, knowing that it serves a greater purpose.

Lord, I thank you for being a provider. I know that you have blessed me and put me right where I am supposed to be. Help me to strive for excellence in everything that I do. May You establish the work of my hands, and may my work reflect Your love. Amen.

Day 13

Eastern Phoebe

"You will keep in perfect peace those whose minds are steadfast, because they trust in you."
– Isaiah 26:3

Another little bird that is known for its calmness is the Eastern Phoebe. Unlike other birds that move in an unpredictable manner, the Phoebe is more poised in the way they carry themselves. They have a unique "fee-bee" sound that distinguishes them from other birds and soothes the environment as they announce their presence. As Isaiah 26:3 reminds us, peace is not found in our circumstances but in a steadfast mind and trust in God. The Phoebe's consistent, peaceful presence illustrates all of these qualities.

Almost daily, we face distractions and worries that can trouble our hearts. The Scriptures clearly emphasize the absolute necessity of running to the Lord in times of trouble and distress to find peace in Him. We are further encouraged to place all our trust in God in order to navigate life's challenges in calmness and peace, just as the Phoebe does. This very knowledge serves as a reminder that God will surely see us through the tough waters amidst any challenge we may be faced with.

Lord, you tell us that you will give us rest when we come to You. Help me to stay afloat in my thoughts and actions so that I can continue to put all my trust in You amidst any difficult situation. Give me peace as I run to you, and guide me to always trust in you alone. You are my refuge, Lord. Amen.

Day 14
Red-bellied Woodpecker

"In all your ways acknowledge Him, and He will make your paths straight." – Proverbs 3:6

A dogged and persistent bird, the Red-bellied Woodpecker will repeatedly tap on trees in search of food or to build a nest. The woodpecker is gifted with a strong beak that allows it to carve out a path for food and home. It is evident that this bird is guided by instinct and purpose. This serves as a reminder we can navigate the paths set before us when we trust in the provision and purpose of God. We can trust in God, even when the paths seem difficult. He is faithful to direct our steps even in the midst of great uncertainty.

Just as the woodpecker relies on its natural gifting to thrive in its environment, we are called to trust that the Lord will guide us, equipping us with all that we need to fulfill our purpose. When we acknowledge Him in all that we do, He will lead us faithfully along the right path.

Lord, help me to acknowledge You in all aspects of my life today. I know that You are worthy and faithful. Guide my steps and give me the perseverance of the Red-bellied Woodpecker, pressing forward in the direction You have set for me. Amen.

Day 15

House Sparrow

"Are not five sparrows sold for two pennies? Yet not one of them is forgotten by God." – Luke 12:6

The House Sparrow is a common, albeit overlooked, sight in virtually every corner of the world. Though small and seemingly insignificant, these birds are hardy survivors who find a way to thrive in the midst of an ever-changing world. In many ways, they remind us of God's care for the "overlooked" and "insignificant." Jesus used the sparrow as an example that no one is actually overlooked or insignificant, reassuring us that no one is forgotten by God.

Much like the sparrow, we may feel like our lives are too ordinary and that our struggles are too small to be noticed by God. However, Jesus promises that we are valued far more than many sparrows. We are seen in every moment, even the unnoticed and unremarkable ones. He cares deeply about each of our needs. When you are tempted to feel overlooked or insignificant, rest assured that God sees and loves you.

Heavenly Father, thank You for the reminder that, much like the sparrow, I am never forgotten by You. Help me to trust in Your ever-present, steady care, even in moments I feel small or insignificant. Amen.

Day 16

Eastern Bluebird

"You make known to me the path of life, you will fill me with joy in your presence, with eternal pleasures at your right hand." – Psalm 16:11

The Eastern Bluebird, with its bright blue feathers, is often spotted sitting atop a telephone wire before abruptly dropping to the ground in pursuit of an insect.

Observing one of these birds seems like a gift, a glimpse into the beauty of God's design. The Eastern Bluebird is a great "bird box" bird, often returning back to the same man-made box. The male bluebird can be observed perched at the opening of the bird box with the hope of attracting a mate.

Just as the bluebird thrives when it finds the perfect nesting place, we find true joy when we find rest in God's presence. We live in a world that overpromises. The only place to find peace that surpasses all understanding and is untethered to our circumstances is in the Lord's will and presence. Everywhere else will eventually let you down. Allow the Eastern Bluebird to remind you to seek God's presence daily and find delight in Him alone.

Lord, please guide my steps in accordance with what Your plan is for me today. Help me find joy in Your presence, trusting in Your provision and finding rest in Your perfect peace. Amen.

Day 17

Brown-headed Cowbird

"As iron sharpens iron, so one person sharpens another." – Proverbs 27:17

The Brown-headed Cowbird is known for *brood parasitism*. This simply means that it will lay its eggs in the nests of other species of birds. Although this may seem strange and even appalling at first glance, it highlights the interconnectedness of creation and design. Cowbirds are also a great example of the value of community and teamwork. They congregate in large flocks and have the ability to adapt to a number of environments.

Much like the cowbird, we, too, should aim to lean on community. Proverbs 27:17 reminds us to sharpen one another and to support each other's growth in our faith journey. Although we shouldn't place our caretaker responsibilities on other people, we should lean on one another for support and guidance. No one was designed to live life alone, and the Brown-headed Cowbird serves as a reminder of the importance of inspiring growth towards Christ within our faith community.

Lord, help me to be a source of encouragement for those around me today. Allow me to sharpen others and inspire growth in You. Praise You for the people you have surrounded me with. Help me not to isolate myself in times of need. Amen.

Day 18
Baltimore Oriole

"Whatever you do, work at it with all your heart,
as working for the Lord, not for human masters."
— Colossians 3:23

One of nature's beauties, the Baltimore Oriole stands out in splendor. Known for its vibrant orange and black feathers, it becomes easily identified when perched on trees, which is an amazing sight to behold. The Baltimore Oriole is known for its creativity in making complex nests. The lesson we can learn from these special creatures is seen in their ability to meticulously carry out their duties with determination, creativity and attention to detail. We can liken these traits to how we, as humans, should value the things we do and work toward achieving them to glorify God's name.

When we consider the effort the orioles put into making their wonderful nests, it serves as a reminder that we should approach every moment with determination and creativity to achieve a common goal. This purpose of aiming for greater things can manifest in our careers, relationships, or in our day-to-day lives. With diligence, just as the Baltimore Oriole, we must utilize every moment to give God glory.

Lord, guide me in your path so I can work with diligence, which will reflect Your glory. May my thoughts and creativity be a reflection of Your goodness and love. Amen.

Day 19

Northern Flicker

"Let the fields be jubilant, and everything in them; let all the trees of the forest sign for joy."
– Psalm 96:12

The Northern Flicker is a true sight to behold, distinguished not only by its vivid colors but also by its unique behavior. Unlike others in the woodpecker family, the flicker does most of its foraging on the ground, looking for ants and other insects. This unique behavior shows that each bird finds its own way to thrive in the place God has set for it. This special bird is a subtle reminder that all of God's creations are designed to worship Him with their unique features.

As seen in the unique qualities of the flicker, we too have been blessed with traits and features that should bring glory to God when properly used. The flicker doesn't behave like other woodpeckers, nor does it conform to the world around it. Likewise, we should embrace our differences as part of God's diverse creation. Just as the flicker's call stands out and adds to the surrounding symphony, we can, too. So, we must ensure to bask in the joy of the wealth of gifts that God has blessed us with - our talents, callings, and passions.

Lord, I thank you for allowing me to know that I'm specially made and different. Guide me to properly use my gifts to praise You and bring glory to your holy name. Amen.

39

Day 20

Summer Tanager

"Taste and see that the Lord is good; blessed is the one who takes refuge in Him." – Psalm 34:8

The Summer Tanager is an amazingly colored bird that is known for its trait of feasting unusually. They are great bee and wasp hunters, which they do effortlessly without considering the dangers attached to them. This trait summarizes their boldness as a unique quality that distinguishes them from other birds. It further illustrates for us that amidst the challenges we may face, when we approach our fears with boldness, we will always reap great rewards.

The Summer Tanager carefully chooses its daily sustenance. Like the Tanager, we are called to seek the Lord first. The world promises much and under delivers. In Psalm 34, the psalmist invites readers to "taste and see" the goodness of God. The Lord is good on His promises to sustain us. We must ensure to seek the Lord first in all our endeavors and then trust that He will make them all available to us. The unique feature of this very bird teaches us just that. Refrain from taking the quickest route. When you put your faith in the Lord, He will sustain you no matter how hard things get.

Lord, I want to seek You first today. I want to experience the sweetness of your faithfulness and protection. Teach me to trust in Your plan for my life, knowing that You will sustain and bless me when I find my refuge in You. Amen.

41

Day 21
Barn Swallow

*"Even the sparrow finds a home, and the swallow
a nest for herself, where she may lay her young."
– Psalm 84:3*

A unique feature of the Barn Swallow that distinguishes
it from other birds is its swift flight patterns and
charming beauty. The name of the bird "Barn Swallow" is
derived from its ability to feed and drink while still in the
air. Their common dwelling place is nesting near barns.
Barn Swallows are great builders that can make their nest
from sand and grass. They have high adaptation features as
they can survive in natural habitats with humans.

It is worthy to note that we can find peace when we make
God our safe haven, just as the Barn Swallow hatchlings
find peace in their mother's nest. God is our great provider
and safety net. He continually reminds us in His Word that
he is always with us. We must put all our trust in Him as we
journey through life's challenges and dark waters.

---

*Lord, thank You for being my place of peace and rest.
Thank You for Your provision that is made available to
us. Just as You have taught me in Your word, continue to
help me to build a place where people can find rest as well.
Amen.*

Day 22
Carolina Chickadee

"Cast all your anxiety on Him because He cares for you." – 1 Peter 5:7

There are some birds that bring a special sense of joy when seen in their environment. The Carolina Chickadee is one such bird. In its flight, it flits effortlessly from branch to branch acrobatically, unconcerned with what tomorrow might bring. Despite its diminutive size, it makes its presence known with its lively spirit and constant chatter. This bird is very approachable and social, making it a steady presence in backyards. Though the chickadee has many daily needs, it is not overly burdened by them. It knows instinctively that those needs will be provided for.

Often we find ourselves burdened and worried about our daily needs. God knows our every need, and we are called to cast all our anxieties on the Lord, knowing that He loves and cares for us. When life feels overwhelming, look to the example of the Chickadee. Be reminded that God's care is steady and sure. Allow this promise to move you to a lifestyle of joy and vigor, like the Chickadee. The Lord will meet your needs, calm your fears, and lift your burdens.

Lord, help me to run to you first when I experience anxiety and worry. Teach me to walk in freedom and joy that only comes from trusting in You. Thank you for caring for me. Amen

Day 23
Mourning Dove

"Blessed are the peacemakers, for they will be called children of God." – Matthew 5:9

The soft cooing of the Mourning Dove is a familiar sound across North America. Often heard at dawn and dusk, their song adds a sense of lament in our backyards and neighborhoods. Also known for its gentle demeanor, this bird symbolizes peace and comfort in many cultures. Its soothing call serves as a reminder that in times of sorrow and distress, we can still find peace that only the Lord can provide. Mourning doves can often be seen in pairs, which is a testament to their devotion to one another. Just as the mourning dove pursues unity, we are called to be peacemakers, bringing unity to the disorder and chaos around us.

We often associate the term peacemaker with blunt force and aggression. The mourning dove's quiet strength reminds us that peacemaking isn't always loud or forceful. It's often found in gentle actions and quiet words, reflecting the attitude of Christ. As we experience conflict in our world, we are called to be champions of reconciliation and kindness. Ensure to be a promoter of peace in today's broken world.

Lord, help me to be a peacemaker today. May I not be passive when I experience injustice, but to pursue peacemaking with the power and gentleness of Christ. Amen.

Day 24

American Crow

"For everything there is a season, and a time for every matter under heaven." – Ecclesiastes 3:1

The American Crow is an intelligent and easily recognizable bird that is known for its all-black appearance and distinctive "caw". Crows have learned to thrive in a wide ranger of environments, from rural farmland to highly urbanized areas. Often found in large groups working together, they showcase their remarkable cognitive ability by solving complex problems.

The crow reminds us that community is crucial in every season. Just as the crow adapts to its ever-changing environment, we too must embrace the different seasons God calls us into. Whether on a mountain top or in a valley, we can trust that God has a purpose for us in every moment and is surrounding us with a community to guide us through every season.

Lord, help me to walk boldly into every season you call me into. May I face trials of every kind with confidence, knowing that You are present and active. Surround me with a community that motivates me to pursue Your plan. Amen.

Day 25

European Starling

"Let each of you look not only to his own interests, but also to the interests of others." – Philippians 2:4

Beautiful and gregarious, the European Starling has iridescent plumage and complex vocal abilities. Murmurations are the distinct feature that these birds possess, often flying in large, elegant flocks. Their harmony and collaboration are on full display in these mesmerizing aerial performances. Despite being an introduced species, starlings have adapted wonderfully and thrive as they cooperate and support one another. Their unity allows them to be better able to hunt for food and adapt to the changing seasons.

Today, we live in a world where promoting personal achievement is the order of the day. The starling is a symbol of the importance of community and putting the needs of others before our own. Likewise, Paul encourages the Philippians to do the same. We should depend on one another and work toward unity, just like starlings do. God did not create man to be alone, and that was never his purpose. May the starling remind you of this truth.

Lord, today may I put the needs of others before my own and live a life of selflessness. Help me find ways to support and encourage others around me, finding joy along the way. Teach me to strive for unity in every situation. Amen.

Day 26
Ruby-throated Hummingbird

"Be still, and know that I am God; I will be exalted among the nations, I will be exalted in the earth."
— Psalm 46:10

The Ruby-throated Hummingbird, with its brilliant, iridescent colors and rapid wingbeats, is constantly in motion, bursting from flower to feeder. Its ability to maneuver in any number of directions with speed is amazing to observe. But even this tiny bird must pause to rest and refuel. Despite its perceived constant activity, the hummingbird is a great reminder of the significance of simply stopping. Though it moves quickly, the bird's energy is sustained by moments of stillness.

In today's world, the simple truth is that it is so easy to get carried away by the busyness of life. When we do not find ways to be still in God's presence, we experience burnout, undue anxiety and a whole host of other problems. It is in those quiet moments that we are reminded of who God is. His strength renews us when we allow Him in. The hummingbird shows us that no matter how busy we are, there is power in pausing to acknowledge God and finding rest in His presence.

Father, help me to make it a priority to be still before you today. In the busyness of life, give me the wisdom and discipline to pause, reflect, and find my strength in You alone. Amen.

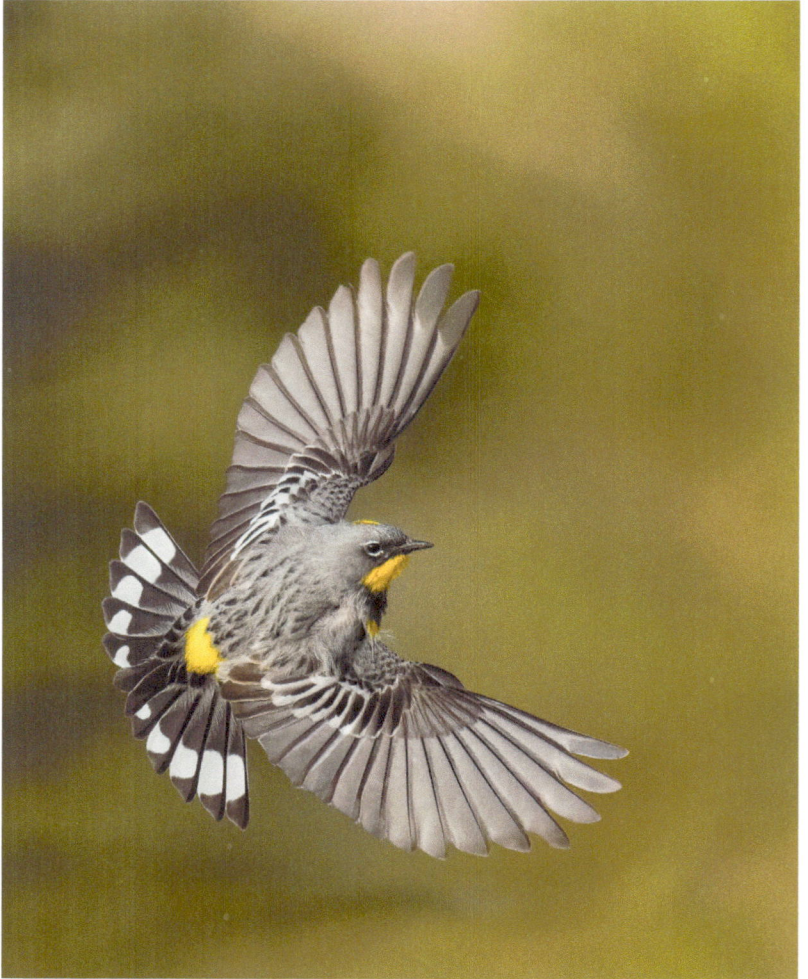

Day 27

Yellow-rumped Warbler

"Your word is a lamp for my feet, a light on my path." – Psalm 119:105

The Yellow-rumped Warbler is a migratory bird that is easily identified by its yellow patch on its underbelly. It travels long distances across North America in sheer volume, adjusting to varying environments, changing seasons, and diets along the way. The warbler reminds us how to approach new or uncertain seasons. They are quick to adapt without changing their features. The Yellow-rumped warbler is prompted along by its instinct, just simply making the next move without hesitation.

Just as the warbler is guided on its journey, scripture reminds us that we, too, are guided along our journey of life. God's word is a lamp unto our feet, lighting the way when life feels uncertain. God promises to help us with the next step. So, we have to trust that He will light each step as we take it. As the warbler trusts its instincts, we can rely on the guidance God has provided via His word and Spirit. He will lead us with wisdom and light each step.

Father, thank you for being the light of the world and promising to illuminate each step I take when I walk with You. Help me to trust in Your direction, even when it seems unclear. Give me confidence to follow You faithfully on the journey You have set before me. Amen.

Day 28
Painted Bunting

"The Lord does not look at the things people look at. People look at the outward appearance, but the Lord looks at the heart." – 1 Samuel 16:7

Known as one of the most beautiful birds you can find in North America, the Painted Bunting is adorned with vibrant rainbow-colored feathers. Its first appearance may seem unreal, but that is simply the uniqueness of their creation. However, it is worthwhile to note that this beautiful creature has other unique traits apart from its beauty. We can also observe its cautious and quiet nature, especially when in its natural habitat. This further highlights that internal beauty should be considered along with external beauty.

When we carefully look at the narrative of this bird, we will find that it highlights how God sees us. He listens to our hearts. Just as the beauty of this bird goes beyond its physical appearance, it reminds us to cultivate and nurture the habit of paying attention to our inward beauty to glorify God.

Lord, help me to focus on what really matters today. I know that outward appearances fade and change. Help my character and attitude reflect Your love and truth, and may I see others as You see them. Amen.

Day 29

Carolina Wren

"Sing to the Lord a new song, sing to the Lord, all the earth." – Psalm 96:1

Carolina Wrens are notorious for their loud, cheery songs, which can be heard in backyards and woods. Their volume often seems out of proportion to the size of the bird. The Bible teaches that regardless of the season, there is always a reason to sing praises to God, and the Carolina Wren epitomizes this truth. The Wren keeps singing its heart out no matter how bad the weather gets.

Regardless of the challenges and trials we may face, like the Wren, we can lift our voices and praise the God who will never leave us. Singing praises to God helps us to lift our eyes above the difficulties of life, bringing us closer to God. Let the Carolina Wren remind us to sing a new song to the Lord each day, a song declaring His goodness and faithfulness.

Father, help me to have a heart of praise in every season, even in the most difficult ones. Teach my heart to sing a new song to You, just as the Carolina Wren fills the world with a joyful noise. Amen.

Day 30
Dark-eyed Junco

"But those who hope in the Lord will renew their strength. They will soar on wings like eagles; they will run and not grow weary, they will walk and not be faint." – Isaiah 40:31

The Dark-eyed Junco is a neat, unassuming bird, often found hopping along the ground in flocks foraging for food. Although it doesn't have the flashy plumage of other songbirds, its distinct slate-gray feathers and cheerful demeanor help it to stand out. The Dark-eyed Junco carries a quiet strength and resilience. We are often drawn to the outlandish beauty or vibrancy of life, but the junco teaches us that sometimes the most remarkable beauty lies in simplicity and steadfastness.

We all face moments riddled by weariness and doubt. Isaiah 40:31 reminds us that the Lord will renew our strength if we place our hope in Him. He is steadfast in nature; therefore, a hope found in Him is unfading. It is a living hope. Jesus assured this by His life, death, and resurrection. Marvel at the beauty of His steadfast and faithful nature.

Lord, help me to evaluate where my hope lies today. Convict me where my hope is misplaced and help me to shift my hope unto You. Renew my strength and grant me the courage to keep running the race set before me. Amen.

Day 31

Northern Mockingbird

"Speaking to one another with psalms, hymns, and songs from the Spirit. Sing and make music from your heart to the Lord." – Ephesians 5:19

The wide and colorful array of melodies produced by the Northern Mockingbird more than compensates for its limited coloration. People celebrate this bird for its ability to mimic the songs of numerous other bird species and non-bird species. The mockingbird actually takes its singing ability a bit further than simple mimicry, blending songs into their own unique performance. Its voice fills the air with variety and beauty, reminding us of the joyful ways in which we can share God's glory.

In like manner, we are called to lift our voices in praise, as Paul lays out in Ephesians. One wonderful thing about praising God is that it has benefits beyond just ourselves. For people in our lives, it is a source of inspiration. Just as the mockingbird's song refreshes the morning air, our praises-rooted in the Word of God and sung with authenticity bring joy to the Lord and strengthen the community of faith.

Lord, help me to sing your praises with enthusiasm and confidence today. May my lifestyle of worship encourage others and glorify You. May my life be a reflection of your joy and love. Amen.

About the Author

Matthew D. Bennett is husband, dad, worship pastor, and birder. He finds deep peace in connecting with God in the beauty of His creation and His word. Whether he is watching a backyard Blue jay or leading a small group through scripture, he's always looking for ways to connect everyday beauty with God's truth.

Matt created *Bird and the Word*, a podcast and devotional series, to help others draw closer to God through both His creation and His Word. This devotional - *A Birder's Devotional: Backyard Edition* - is the first of many projects that brings those passions together.

Matt lives with his wife and four kids, whom he frequently reminds: "Go find a bird."

www.ingramcontent.com/pod-product-compliance
Lightning Source LLC
Chambersburg PA
CBHW041916260326
41914CB00013B/1473